More than...
ONE OVER THE EIGHT

DERIVATIONS OF EVERYDAY WORDS AND EXPRESSIONS

COMPILED BY

TONY WOOTTON AND GWEN ZANZOTTERA

ILLUSTRATIONS BY

Drawing the Line

All rights reserved. No part of this book may be reproduced or used in any form or by any means, electronic or mechanical, including photocopying, or by any information storage and retrieval system, without permission in writing from the publishers.

© Anthony Wootton and Gwenette Zanzottera

Illustrations by Drawing the Line
Printed by Vale Print & Design (Willersey)

Published by
Wootton-Zanzottera
Email: GWENETTEZAN@aol.com

G Zanzottera
18 Childs Close
STRATFORD UPON AVON
01789 299486
CV37 0TG

FOREWORD

Following the success of their book **By Hook or By Crook**, published in July 2000, which has already sold many thousands of copies and is still selling well, Tony Wootton and Gwen Zanzottera have decided to publish another book of sayings and their origins.

Tony and Gwen are Heart of England qualified Blue Badge Guides who are often asked for the origins of the sayings which they use on their tours. Most of these are sayings or unusual words which are part and parcel of our language.

Their last book also included widely used quotations from Shakespeare - this book has quotations from other authors and sources.

Tony and Gwen would like to thank Graham Robson of 'Drawing the Line' who contributed to the huge success of their first book by putting his individual style and great humour into the illustrations, as he has continued to do with this new book **One Over the Eight**.

Also, their grateful thanks go to Vale Press who were so helpful in all aspects of the printing of both books.

Tracing the derivations has again been intriguing and enjoyable. Tony Wootton and Gwen Zanzottera hope that you find their new book equally intriguing and enjoyable.

All men by nature desire knowledge.
(Aristotle)

AN AXE TO GRIND

We often say that we wonder if a person has **an axe to grind** when someone is very persuasive about following a particular course of action, and we suspect them of having an ulterior motive.

The saying dates back to the days of Benjamin Franklin, the American inventor. He used to tell the story of when he was very young, a man carrying an axe came into the yard where he was working and asked him to show the man how the grindstone worked. Benjamin took a lot of trouble showing the man how the blade should be ground properly, and when he had finished the man laughed and left - carrying his nice sharp axe.

BARBECUE

The summer breeze is blowing, the midges are biting, the charcoal is glowing or the gas bottle is hissing and the chicken or the steaks are sizzling on the barbecue. But where does the word **barbecue** come from?

There are two possible definitions. One is from barbacoa, a word from Haiti meaning a framework of sticks set upon poles. However, the more likely one is from France where an animal such as an ox was roasted whole, from the head to the tail, the French for which is **barbe á queue**.

THE BEST MAN

Nowadays the best man at the wedding is the one who arranges the cars and drops the wedding ring and who makes one of the speeches at the wedding.

"... at a time like this, your asking if I've got the RING"

The tradition of the best man at the wedding goes back many years to Scotland and the practice of carrying off the woman a man was in love with, often in the face of opposition and fighting from her family.

The groomsmen, or friends of the bridegroom, would all help in this abduction, and the best and bravest of his friends was always known as the **best man**.

BETWEEN THE DEVIL AND THE DEEP BLUE SEA

Some of the sayings associated with the devil are obvious, for instance when we tell someone to **go to the devil** we are saying that we really do not care what happens to him.

However, when a person is in a difficult situation and whichever solution they choose is likely to lead to trouble, we say that they are **between the devil and the deep blue sea**. This saying goes back to sailing ships and the devil in this case was a heavy beam on the side of a ship, helping to support the big guns. It was a difficult place to get to and rather precarious so if a sailor had to work on this beam he had to take great care not to fall off into the sea.

BOB'S YOUR UNCLE

When something goes well or when everything is expected to turn out fine, people often say 'Bob's your uncle',

Surprisingly, this saying has a political background and is said to come from the fact that in 1900 the Conservative Party leader Robert Cecil picked his nephew for an important government position. The appointment was very unpopular at the time and was said to have come about because of the family connection - Bob was his uncle.

CATHERINE WHEEL

This is usually used to describe a firework in the shape of a wheel and which spins on a central nail fastening it to a door or post.

It does in fact date back to the 4th Century and St Catherine of Alexandria who publicly confessed to the Christian faith at a sacrificial feast. She was ordered to be tortured on a wheel but miraculously escaped.

The fool wonders, the wise man asks.
(Benjamin Disraeli)

A CHANGELING

For hundreds of years, all babies were dressed in nighgowns and then dresses. Once they reached the age of two or a little older, little boys were put into the more usual trousers and shirts.

Although it went on right into the twentieth century, this is a practice which dates back to the Middle Ages when people believed in fairies and witches. In those days, it was thought that the bad fairies took away healthy and well-nourished babies to fairyland and left a thin and miserable baby, or **changeling** in its place. For some reason, it was thought that only boys were taken and this is why all babies were dressed as girls - to confuse the fairies.

"Alice... you're not fooling ANYBODY"

A thing of beauty is a joy for ever.
(John Keats)

CHEWING THE FAT

This is sometimes used to describe people just talking and may have come from Cockney rhyming slang for having a chat.

It is more likely to have come from the days of sailing ships when the only way of preserving meat for long voyages was to put the meat into barrels of salt. This made the meat very hard and chewy and it took a long time to eat.

At that time sailors lived and worked in very harsh conditions, and if they were seen to be slacking or wasting time talking and grumbling while they should have been working, the punishments were severe. The only time they could get together was when they were eating and the long time taken to chew the hard fat could be a cover for the fact that they were talking and not working.

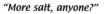
"More salt, anyone?"

Heart of oak are our ships.
(David Garrick)

A CHIP ON YOUR SHOULDER

When someone is argumentative, sulky or saying that everyone is picking on them, we say that they have **a chip on their shoulder.**

This saying came from America and started about 200 years ago. When schoolboys were spoiling for a fight, one boy would pick up a chip of wood and place it on this shoulder. He would challenge the other to knock it off and this would start the fight.

CLIMB ON THE BANDWAGON

If someone takes advantage of a situation and benefits from it, or shares in the publicity or praise for something without deserving it, we say that they have **'climbed on the bandwagon'**

This comes from the southern states of America when a wagon with a band on it would go through the streets in front of the circus or to publicise religious or political meetings. Whenever there was an election the candidates or people in support would climb on the bandwagon, thus knowing that they would be noticed and so obtain plenty of publicity.

There are three kinds of lies - lies, damned lies and statistics. (Mark Twain)

CLINKING DRINKING GLASSES TOGETHER

People drinking wine usually clink their glasses together and say 'Cheers' or 'Good health'.

One explanation, from France, is that the clink of the glasses completes the use of the five senses when having a drink. The wine is poured and the sense of sight is used in looking at the colour of the wine, the sense of smell when enjoying the bouquet of the wine, the sense of touch when holding a fine wineglass. Although the sense of taste will be used later in enjoying the wine, before that the sense of hearing is used in clinking the glasses in good fellowship.

However, it is thought in some circles to originate in Italian history when noblemen were often sworn enemies. The Borgias were not the only family poisoning their enemies and visiting noblemen were deeply suspicious of their hosts. The wine was poured then a little wine from one nobleman's glass poured into another so that both hosts and guests drank the same mixture. As this was taking place, the glasses often clinked as they touched and this is where the practice started of clinking glasses and drinking a toast to good health.

A COCKNEY

This is often used to describe anyone who comes from London, particularly someone with a strong dialect.

The term 'cockney' originally meant someone whose experience and knowledge were exclusively from the town, (what we might call 'streetwise'), and even today in the United States the word means a townsman.

Strictly speaking, however, a **cockney** is someone who was born within the sound of Bow bells, i.e. within the sound of the bells of the Church of St Mary le Bow in London.

CODSWALLOP

When someone is saying something which is far-fetched or rubbish, we often say they are talking **'a load of old codswallop'**.

This is another saying from America where in 1875 Hiram Codd patented a special bottle of mineral water, which became very popular, but not with hardened beer drinkers.

Alcoholic drinks, especially beer, were often called 'wallop', and Codd's Wallop' was used in a sarcastic way to describe this mineral water. This became **'codswallop'** and eventually came to mean anything inferior or false.

Work is the curse of the drinking classes.
(Oscar Wilde)

CROCODILE TEARS

This is a saying used when someone is pretending to be sad or remorseful when in reality they are not.

It comes from the old belief that crocodiles shed tears when they kill for food, which in turn comes from the fact that crocodiles have very large tear glands and when they are fighting to kill something, the agitation or over-excitement makes the tears flow.

DOGS

There are many sayings associated with dogs. If we follow someone closely we say we **dog their footsteps**, rather like a dog following its master

If a book is **dog-eared** it means that the crumpled corners resemble the limp and downturned ears of a dog.

When one is **dog tired**, one flops down in a heap rather like a dog in front of the fire.

I cried all the way to the bank.
(Liberace)

DON'T COUNT YOUR CHICKENS

People are often told 'don't count your chickens before they are hatched' when explaining how a plan is going to succeed or how much money they are going to make out of a particular venture.

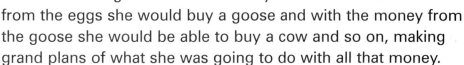

This saying goes back to one of Aesop's fables and is the story of a woman who was taking a basket of eggs to market. As she walked along she was thinking that with the money from the eggs she would buy a goose and with the money from the goose she would be able to buy a cow and so on, making grand plans of what she was going to do with all that money.

Unfortunately, she was not concentrating on where she was going and she tripped over, breaking all the eggs in the basket and so all her plans came to nothing.

A DOSSHOUSE

A dosshouse is a name for a very run down hostel for poor people and vagrants to sleep in, and this type of hostel was very common in the 1920s and 1930s. 'Doss' is an Elizabethan word meaning a hassock or a mattress stuffed with straw and this was the type of mattress which was common in these old hostels.

We still use the phrase **to doss down** if someone is going to stay overnight and they have to sleep on the floor because there are no beds available.

DRESSED TO THE NINES

When someone is really dressed up, particularly for a special occasion, we say that that are **'dressed to the nines'**.

The origins of this are obscure but it could possibly have come from the expression 'dressed to the eyne', a very old word meaning eyes. If you were dressed up to the eyes, it meant that you were smartly dressed from head to foot and it is easy to see how, before the days of written language when sayings were just spoken, dressed to the eynes became dressed to the nines.

THE FAT IS IN THE FIRE

If someone makes a careless remark which might spark off a quarrel or a disagreement, we say that **the fat is in the fire now.**

When meat was being cooked on a spit or fried in a pan over the fire, it was essential that the grease or fat did not fall into the fire otherwise the fire would blaze and smoke and so spoil the taste of the food. A sudden blaze could be likened to tempers flaring up.

All dressed up, with nowhere to go.
(William White)

A FEATHER IN YOUR CAP

If you succeed in something difficult or win a battle, people will say **'that's a feather in your cap'** meaning that is an honour to you.

This comes from the practice in Asia, and, more particularly, with the native Americans, of adding a feather to their head-dress for every enemy they have killed.

A HAIR OF THE DOG

Anyone with a bad hangover from having drunk too much the night before is often advised the following morning to have another alcoholic drink or **'a hair of the dog which bit you'**.

This comes from the old belief that the burnt hair of a dog is a cure for its bite. Sadly, neither cure seems to work.

Nothing is certain but death and taxes.
(Benjamin Franklin)

"Never again....."

HIGGLEDY PIGGLEDY

When things are all in a muddle, or thrown in a heap, we say that they are all **'higgledy piggledy'**.

A higgler was a peddler, a man who went from place to place selling things such as ribbons or pots and pans, and his stores were often all tumbled together in the peddler's basket. Piggledy comes from a pig's litter, and refers to the way in which the piglets lie along the sow to be fed, often all muddled up and lying on top of one another. The two words were used together because of the matching sound of **higgledy piggledy**.

HIGH JINKS

This is often used to describe riotous or boisterous behaviour. A 'jink' was a word for a jump and probably referred to people being in high spirits and jumping about, particularly when drunk.

There was also a game called **'high jinks'** which was played at one time in Scottish taverns. People played various parts and if they failed, they had to pay a forfeit.

Let them eat cake.
(Marie Antoinette on hearing that the people had no bread to eat)

HOIST WITH YOUR OWN PETARD

This is often used where someone has hatched a clever and devious plan which goes wrong and lands that person in trouble.

It comes from the days when a petard (a barrel or case filled with explosives) was used for blowing in the door of a castle or fortified place.   The fuse to the explosive was sometimes too short and the attacker was then blown up by his own explosive.

TO HOODWINK

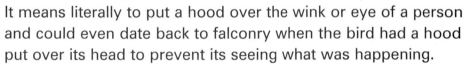

This is an expression often used when someone is being deceived or 'hoodwinked'. It means literally to put a hood over the wink or eye of a person and could even date back to falconry when the bird had a hood put over its head to prevent its seeing what was happening.

TO KNOCK OFF

Often used when someone is finishing a job or, more particularly, a shift.

In the cotton mills in the north of England, the machines were run by a continuous belt running over pulleys. When you finished your shift, you knocked the belt off the pulleys and the machines came to a halt.

"I'll 'ave to get a longer pole ... I've not stopped working in three weeks"

A LAPDOG

Someone who is made a fuss of is often referred to as a **lapdog**, and the picture comes to mind of a sweet little dog sitting in the lap of a lady and being pampered and petted.

However, in the Middle Ages lapdogs served another purpose and that was to rid a lady of her fleas. Everyone, from royalty downwards, had fleas and ladies used to keep their little dog on their lap, not on top of their skirts but on their bare knees. The fleas preferred the blood heat of the little dog and so jumped off the lady and into the fur of the dog. After a while, when the dog was put outside, it took all the fleas with it.

MIND ONE'S Ps and Qs

This expression is used when someone has to be careful what they say, particularly when going into high society or a difficult situation.

It is thought to be connected to the pub trade. Many poor people had a **'slate'** and this was literally a piece of slate which hung behind the bar. Every drink they had was written on the slate with a piece of chalk and at the end of the week, when they were paid, all the drinks were added up and the bill was settled.

It was important to be accurate when adding up the money owing and not to confuse the pints, which were chalked up as P's with the quarts (two pints) which were chalked up as Q's. . (Even today, people will often say **'put it on the slate'** when they want credit in a pub or small shop and then they will settle the bill at the end of the week).

ON THE DOLE

Although we associate being on the dole with the twentieth century, and particularly with the recession of the early 1920s, this goes back hundred of years.

It applies particularly to villages and small communities. The more wealthy people in that community would give food to feed the very poor, and as the Church was the centre of village life at that time, this food would be taken to the local Church to be distributed.

The food would be collected in a **dole** chest and the poor people would come to the Church and stand in line for the food to be **doled out**

Dole comes from the Anglo Saxon 'dal' meaning a portion or a share, and is also connected with 'to deal' which also means to share out, particularly in card games.

Food, glorious food
(Lionel Bart)

ONE OVER THE EIGHT

Someone who has drunk too much is often referred to as having had **one over the eight**.

This dates back to the Middle Ages when everyone drank ale.   Very small babies drank a weak form of ale called small ale or 'tilly willy'.   Children of seven were drinking full strength ale and a woman would drink about six pints a day. A man, however, would usually drink eight pints and after that he was considered drunk and, therefore, unfit for work.

If he was found drunk, he had certainly had **one over the eight**.

PANCAKE DAY

Shrove Tuesday, the day before the start of Lent, is often known as Pancake Day.   Lent is the season of fasting in many Christian Churches and lasts for 40 days and 40 nights.   The pancakes cooked on Pancake Day used up all the rich ingredients which could not be used during Lent and which, in fact, would have gone bad if left until after Easter.

This practice began in the days when people were relatively poor and could not afford to waste any food and also, of course, there were no fridges or even larders and so no means of keeping perishable foods for any length of time.

Incidentally the word Shrove comes from being shriven of one's sins, in other words going to Church to confess one's sins and then fasting through Lent in penitence.

PILLAR TO POST

When people go chasing in all directions without making any actual progress and without achieving anything, we often say that they are going **from pillar to post**.

This saying goes back to horse management. The pillar was in the centre of the riding ground in a riding school and the posts were columns, usually in pairs, at equal distances round the riding ring. Training the horse to go **'from pillar to post'** was training it to go from the centre pillar to the posts round the edge and back again. It was just an exercise in training and did not mean that they were reaching a destination or goal.

PIN MONEY

Pin money is the spending money which a husband used to allow to his wife for spending on herself. It is quite separate from money for housekeeping and dates back to when the pins which women used to fasten collars together or to pin scarves or ribbons onto their dresses were often made of silver and, therefore, very expensive.

Women could often not afford to buy them for themselves, and would apply to their husbands for 'pin money'.

A little of what you fancy does you good.
(Marie Lloyd - a popular Music Hall singer)

A POTHOLE

Whenever we drive over an uneven part of the road or there is a hole in the surface of the road, we say that we are driving over **potholes**.

It is said that, where roads were just rough tracks - particularly where the ground was mostly clay - people would dig up a lump of clay and take it home to make household pots, so leaving a hole in the road.

PUT A SOCK IN IT

When we want someone to be quiet we often say **put a sock in it**.

This goes back to the early days of gramophones when the sound used to come out of a large horn. There was no knob to make the sound louder or softer, and often the only way to make the sound softer was, literally, to put a sock (or two!) inside the horn. It was certainly a very unorthodox form of volume control.

Scarce, sir, mighty scarce.
(Mark Twain - on being asked what men would become in a world without women)

TO QUEUE

Americans stand in line, but British people queue - usually in a very orderly fashion.

The word **queue** is French for a tail and when one looks at a long line of people waiting for a shop to open or to get into a theatre, it does look just like a long tail.

In the days when all Chinese men had their hair in a pigtail, this pigtail was also known as a queue.

A QUID

This is used nowadays in Britain to mean a £ but originally meant a gold sovereign and was first used in the 19th century: it can also be used to mean cash generally as in the saying 'quids in' meaning 'in the money' or gaining money.

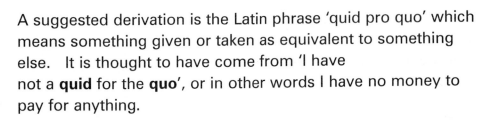

Sick squid

A suggested derivation is the Latin phrase 'quid pro quo' which means something given or taken as equivalent to something else. It is thought to have come from 'I have not a **quid** for the **quo**', or in other words I have no money to pay for anything.

The only place where success comes before work is a dictionary.
(Vidal Sassoon)

RAINING CATS AND DOGS

Various countries have descriptions for very heavy rain - for instance in Germany it is described as raining pipe stems. In England we often talk of **raining cats and dogs**.

Witches who rode on broomsticks during rainstorms were supposed to take the form of a cat and in Northern mythology the cat is supposed to have a great influence on the weather. Dogs are often thought of in connection with the wind, particularly in Norse mythology. The wind was often pictured in old German pictures as coming from the mouth of a dog or even a wolf.

"Typical April ... has been raining humans all day"

The cat signifies the rain and the dog a wind so a bad rainstorm with strong wind is summed up as 'raining cats and dogs'.

RATS TAILS

A rats tail is a thin dangling lock of hair which obviously resembles the tail of a rat and when someone's hair is very untidy and obviously uncombed we say that the hair is in rats tails.

There are all sorts of stories concerning rats and hair and they may have arisen from the other meaning of the word 'rat' which was a large pad of artificial hair used to make a hairdo look much bigger and more elaborate, particularly in Edwardian times.

A RED LETTER DAY

Any day which is important is known as a **'red letter day'**.

This saying goes back to the practice of printing calendars and almanacs with the Saints days and public holidays in red, while the ordinary days of the week were printed in black.

TO RULE THE ROOST

To **rule the roost** usually means to be the head of the household and to order the way things are done, often in a domineering way. It was at one time thought to have come from 'rule the roast' because the roast meat was always placed in front of the head of the house: he was responsible for carving the meat and working out how much each member of his family was allowed

On the other hand, perhaps it actually came from the henhouse where the cockerel, the male bird, decided which of the hens would share his roost or perch, and therefore he ruled the roost.

SABOTAGE

To **sabotage** something is to make a plan go wrong or, more usually, to wreck machinery and is a word which is used more commonly in time of war or revolution.

".. and remember... take the foot OUT first"

It is another of those sayings which has its origins in a French word, this time a sabot or wooden clog worn by French peasants. If they wanted to wreck machinery they threw a sabot into the machinery and this would damage it, often beyond repair.

A SANDWICH

In the reign of George III the Earl of Sandwich was known as a great gambler who would often spend days on end at the gaming tables. He did not stop for meals and often asked a waiter to bring him meat between two slices of bread and this is where we get the word 'sandwich'.

SHEETING DOWN WITH RAIN

We are not sure of this, but do wonder if it comes from the time when Malta was part of the British Empire. Many English people went there and heard what was said when it rained.

"... Gran, it's raining!!"
[How to make a Maltese cross]

The Maltese word for rain is **Xita**, pronounced Shiita. One can imagine what all the little old ladies in Malta shout when it suddenly starts to rain!

A SKINFLINT

A skinflint is a very mean person who would do anything to save money or be very exacting in making a bargain.

The original term was a 'skin a flint' and meant someone who would try to make use of something as worthless as the skin from a flint, which was a sharp stone used for cutting or for producing a spark.

TO SLEEP ON A CLOTHES LINE

People often say that they are so tired they **could sleep on a clothes line**, in other words they could lean over a washing line and go to sleep.

Although this sounds rather silly and extremely uncomfortable, in the nineteenth century in big cities such as London the very poor and homeless did actually sleep in that way.

The hostels used to charge a couple of pence for a bed (which was an iron frame with a dirty mattress on), or you could pay some very small amount, such as a halfpenny, to sleep on the line. This meant that you slept hanging over a line stretched across the room and when it was time to get up, the owner of the hostel just untied the line and everyone fell in a heap on the floor.

SMALL FRY

People of no importance are often referred to as **'small fry'**.

This has nothing to do with cooking food in a pan, but refers to the young of fish. Fry is a collective name for young fish, particularly those which have just spawned, and now as well as meaning people it can also mean things of little or no importance.

A kiss without a moustache is like an egg without salt.
(old Spanish saying)

SON OF A GUN

In the days of sailing ships it was usual for women to be allowed on board for various purposes on the long voyages.

It was not unusual for these women to become pregnant, and when they went into labour a temporary

"Still no idea who the father is then?"

maternity ward was made by stretching a tarpaulin between two of the guns.   In a lot of cases they were not sure who was the father of the child, and so the birth certificate would state simply **'son of a gun'**   Occasionally, the child would be given the surname Gunn.

SOUND AS A BELL

Anything which is perfect for its use is called 'as sound as a bell', and uses 'sound' as meaning perfect, not as a noise.

The phrase was first used in the 17th century and comes from the fact that a cracked bell will not give a note and is, therefore, useless.

Reports of my death are greatly exaggerated.
(Mark Twain on hearing that his obituary had been published)

A SPINSTER

Any unmarried woman is usually referred to as a spinster (occasionally it is used in an unflattering way).

The word **spinster** dates back to Anglo Saxon times when it was the job of the daughters of the household to spend the winter spinning the fleece which had been sheared from the sheep in the summer. This job usually fell to the eldest daughter of the household, and when she married it was the job of the next eldest, and so on. So, when each of the daughters went off to be married she was described in the Parish Register as a 'spinster'.

Incidentally, we use the word **bachelor** to describe an unmarried man and this comes from the old French word *bachilier* which meant an unmarried man aspiring to knighthood. The feminine form of this was bachilette which obviously is never used, and anyhow spinster sounds much more descriptive.

Also, the term **wife** is connected to 'spinster' because it comes from the Saxon word *wefan* meaning to weave. A spinster spun the thread to be used in weaving her wedding clothes (and sometimes household fabric), whereas a wife was one who had already woven her allotted task.

Familiarity breeds contempt - and children.
(Mark Twain)

A SQUARE MEAL

When someone has a plate piled high with food we say that they are having a good square meal.

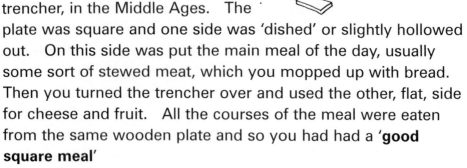

This comes from the use of the wooden plate, or trencher, in the Middle Ages. The plate was square and one side was 'dished' or slightly hollowed out. On this side was put the main meal of the day, usually some sort of stewed meat, which you mopped up with bread. Then you turned the trencher over and used the other, flat, side for cheese and fruit. All the courses of the meal were eaten from the same wooden plate and so you had had a **'good square meal'**

Bread in those days was not always round but usually square and if you were very poor and could not afford a wooden trencher, you had a thick slice of bread with the stew piled on it - still a square meal.

Referring back to the wooden trencher, **a good trencherman** in those days was someone with a good appetite. Also, in some parts of America in the days of the early settlers, there was a disease called **trench mouth**, which happened when a splinter (picked up from licking a wooden trencher to gain the last scraps of food), became embedded in the mouth or tongue and caused an infection.

The rolling English drunkard made the rolling English road.
(Chesterton)

STEEPLECHASE

This is now used to describe a race where the runners (either horses or people) have to jump over obstacles.

Steeplechases first started with a group of foxhunters who were disappointed when they had not caught anything but still had plenty of energy. They could see the steeple of the village church and agreed to race the two miles to it, the winner being the first to touch the church with his whip.

The race was over fields, hedges and ditches and this is where the tradition of a race over obstacles came from.

Sometimes the races are run between two churches and are referred to as **point to point** races, not because they are run from one place to another, but because they are run from one church with a pointed steeple to another.

SWAN SONG

This is often used to describe a musician's last work or an actor's last role.

It comes from the myth that a swan would go somewhere peaceful to die and would always sing just before it died, so the swan's song was the last thing it did.

No one knows where this idea came from but it has been believed for many hundreds of years.

TOUCH AND GO

This is often used where a situation has been hazardous or someone has had a narrow escape or even where someone may or may not survive, particularly in the case of serious illness.

It comes from driving, particularly carriage driving, and relates to when two vehicles were passing on a narrow street and the wheel of one vehicle touched another without doing any actual damage or overturning either vehicle. In other words, there was a touch but both vehicles were able to drive away.

TRUE BLUE

Although often used to describe someone in political terms, the origins of this description of honesty and fidelity were not from politics.

It comes from 'Coventry blue', a blue thread which originated in the city of Coventry and which was particularly noted for the fastness of its dye and for its lasting properties.

Any colour so long as it's black.
(Henry Ford - on the choice of colour for the Model T Ford car)

TWO STRINGS TO HIS BOW

If someone has two jobs, or money invested in two enterprises, we often say that they have 'two strings to their bow'.

This obviously dates back to archery when a broken bowstring could mean the difference between life and death. Archers often had two strings so that if one broke, there was a second string to rely on.

The term **second string** is also used to describe a reserve team of athletes or horses.

WALKING UNDER A LADDER

To walk under a ladder has always been considered unlucky, and the logical explanation would be the fear of something falling on you, for example a pot of paint or a tool being used by the person at the top of the ladder.

This superstition actually comes from more religious times when it was thought that a triangle represented God the Father, God the Son and God the Holy Ghost.

A ladder against a wall obviously makes a triangle and in those days it was thought that to walk through the triangle was breaking up the holy representation and, therefore, unlucky.

I can resist everything except temptation.
(Oscar Wilde)

TO WHET THE APPETITE

This is usually misquoted as to **wet** the appetite, and is often believed to be associated with the practice of wetting a stone when sharpening a blade.

It does in fact come from the Old English *hwettan* or *hwaet* meaning sharp. From this we get the word whetstone which is a stone used to sharpen and so anything which sharpens or intensifies ones appetite is said to **whet the appetite**.

WORKING TO A DEADLINE

When something has to be finished by a certain date, we often say that we are **working to a deadline**. In some jobs, for instance journalism, if work is not in on time the story is 'dead' or useless.

In military prisons, particularly in the American Civil War, there was often a line painted round the boundary and this was known as the 'deadline' because any prisoner crossing this line was shot dead, with no warning.

Another nice mess you've gotten me into.
(Oliver Hardy - of Laurel and Hardy)

YE OLDE TEA SHOPPE

Visitors to the British Isles often see signs for **Ye Olde** shop or tea rooms and believe that this name means that they are in fact very old premises. This may be the case, but very often the title is used because the owners believe that this is how 'the old' was written in the Middle Ages.

Until the end of the Middle Ages the letters 'th' were written in manuscripts as a single character which looked rather like our present day 'y'. When printing was invented, the letter 'y' was available and so came to be used when the old texts were transcribed and so **the** became **ye**.

This practice has persisted through the ages and now is used wherever something is meant to look old.

Have nothing in your houses that you do not know to be useful, or believe to be beautiful.
(William Morris)